JOURNEYS ON THE MISSISSIPPI

JULIAN MESSNER

NEW YORK

JOURNEYS ON THE MISSISSIPPI

by
KAY COOPER

Illustrated with photographs and maps

Published by Julian Messner, a Simon & Schuster
Division of Gulf & Western Corporation, Simon &
Schuster Building, 1230 Avenue of the Americas,
New York, N.Y. 10020.

JULIAN MESSNER and colophon are trademarks of
Simon & Schuster, registered in the U.S.
Patent and Trademark Office.

Manufactured in the United States of America

Design by VIRGINIA M. SOULE

Library of Congress Cataloging in Publication Data

Cooper, Kay.
Journeys on the Mississippi.

Includes index.
SUMMARY: The descriptions of seven journeys down the Mississippi between 1498 and 1980 point out how the river and the valley it runs through have changed.
1. Mississippi River—Description and travel—Juvenile literature. 2. Mississippi River—History—Juvenile literature. 3. Mississippi Valley—Description and travel—Juvenile literature. 4. Mississippi Valley—History—Juvenile literature. [1. Mississippi. 2. Mississippi Valley] I. Title.

F351.C693 917.7'04 80-28109
ISBN 0-671-34024-7

For Mary Catherine Doll

Books by Kay Cooper

JOURNEYS ON THE MISSISSIPPI
"C'MON DUCKS!"
ALL ABOUT GOLDFISH AS PETS
ALL ABOUT RABBITS AS PETS
A CHIPMUNK'S INSIDE-OUTSIDE WORLD

Contents

Acknowledgments

The author acknowledges the kind assistance of the following people:

Wayne C. Temple, deputy director, Illinois State Archives, Springfield, Illinois, for his research on Indians and Jolliet and for his assistance in developing the Lincoln narrative.

Keith Schnepp, architect, Springfield, Illinois, for his use of his research materials on Fort de Chartres.

John and Maxine Nolan, of Springfield, for their photographs.

Peter Westenberger, of Springfield, for his assistance in developing the World War II aspects of the towboat narrative.

Note to the Reader:

This book uses the present names of states, cities, rivers, lakes, and oceans to make it easier to locate them on the maps.

Lake Itasca
Wisconsin
Wisconsin River
Minneapolis
Minnesota
LAKE MICHIGAN
Iowa River
Des Moines River
Muscatine
Rock Island
Chicago
Fort Madison
Louisiana
Hannibal
Iowa
Illinois River
Illinois
Kaskaskia River
Missouri
St. Louis
Fort de Chartres
Missouri River
Ohio River
Cairo
Kentucky
New Madrid
Arkansas
Osceola
Tennessee
Arkansas River
Memphis
Mississippi
Vicksburg
Louisiana
Natchez
Baton Rouge
New Orleans
GULF OF MEXICO

1

Indian Journey
1498

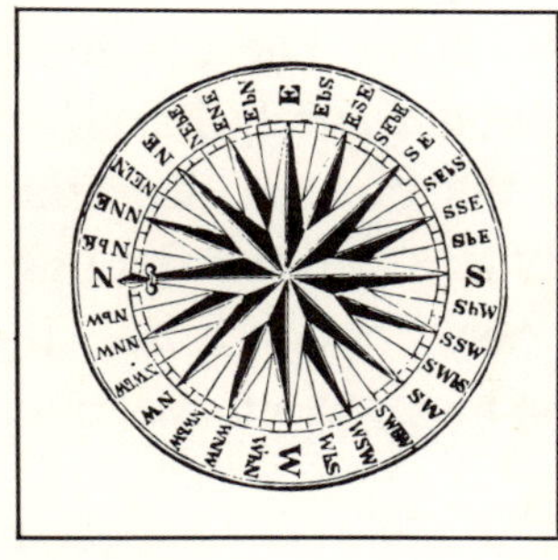

In the spring, a chilly wind swept over a long section of the Mississippi River and stirred up foaming white waves. Trees on the shoreline swayed and creaked. Far in the distance, thunder rumbled. Then the rains poured down on the river and surrounding land.

Suddenly, a bolt of lightning speared through a tree and cut it in half. The tree fell into the river and was swept downstream. Only the stump remained.

Thunderstorms roared over the river for three days, then moved away. The heavy rains caused the Mississippi to flood and spill over the countryside. Animals raced for higher ground. Some became trapped, unable to escape the flood. They

◄

The Mississippi, from its source at Lake Itasca, bending and twisting to its mouth at the Gulf of Mexico. (Map by Mauri Formigoni)

drowned as the river buried bushes and reached five feet up the trunks of big trees.

Along the shoreline where the tree had fallen, the river rose and gnawed into the bank until it collapsed. Chunks of brown earth foamed on the current. Water spun around the tree stump.

A month later, the river was still swollen, moving around and between patches of land that were actually part of the shoreline. Down the river sped a willow-branch canoe covered with animal skins. The lone Indian paddling it was named Tomero. He was a muscular man with dark eyes and black hair.

Tomero struggled bravely with his paddle, trying to keep the canoe in midstream, away from the dangerous rushing currents that kept pulling him closer to the shore. The currents, sweeping along both sides of the river, would surely bash his canoe against tree stumps or rocks on the bottom near the shore. Tomero was also trying desperately to avoid the floating masses of logs and branches that could easily punch a hole in his canoe. If that happened, he would lose his precious cargo to the raging river.

Tomero was a trader, and his canoe was always packed with goods for other Indian tribes. Today, in the spring of 1498, he carried red pipestones from the Minnesota Country. Pipestone was a hard clay which Indians used to make tobacco pipes. Tomero was taking his goods far to the south where the Choctaw Indians lived in Louisiana. He planned to trade the Minnesota pipestones for Choctaw conch shells which were treasured by his people. The seashells, with their beautiful spiral lines, were found in the Gulf of Mexico, far from Tomero's home.

Tomero was a member of a confederation of tribes known as the Iliniwek, which means "people" or "men." The Iliniwek lived throughout central North America, on land bounded by the Wisconsin, Ohio, Wabash and Mississippi rivers. Tomero's village was near the mouth of the Kaskaskia River in Illinois Country.

One day, the name Iliniwek would be changed by white people who often found it difficult to pronounce Indian names. The French traders, who would be the first to meet Tomero's people, would add their French ending "ois" to the word "ilini," thus creating the word "Illinois." This word would be used to name a river and a state.

When Tomero started on his journey, he did not expect the Mississippi to be so dangerous. But far away in the Rocky Mountains and in the vast forests and wide prairies, the spring sun had begun to melt the winter's load of snow. The lakes, which were frozen during the winter, had begun to thaw, too. The heavy spring rains had added their water to the lakes and rivers already swollen with meltwater. And in central North America, the rivers of nearly half the continent have only one place in which to pour all their water—the Mississippi River, the largest and longest of them all.

Although Tomero's people had a name for the river, it was not Mississippi. Many historians believe the present-day name may come from the language of the Choctaw people. The Choctaw name for the river sounded like *meact chassipi* (may-act-chah-sipi), which meant "ancient father of waters." White people gradually changed the name and the spelling until it became Mississippi.

Out of the rich soil near the Mississippi grew plants such as prairie dock and blazing star. These plants and others made up the Illinois prairie near Tomero's village. The prairies existed until the white settlers came to plow

the land and grow crops. In the prairies lived the prairie chicken (far left), Bobwhite quail (background left), buffalo, and cowbird (right). Today, the prairie chicken may disappear forever. (Courtesy of Illinois State Museum)

The Ojibway Indians of the north had the word *mesipi,* which meant "big river." This may also be the origin of the name.

In the year 1498, like many years before and since, more water flowed into the great river during the spring than it could hold. It overflowed its banks onto the land all around.

And in the main channel, where Tomero was fighting the currents, the water was moving fast and carrying along logs and branches. As his canoe heaved and rolled with the waves, Tomero could feel the pull of the powerful current. Skillfully, he kept his canoe in the middle of the main channel and let the rushing water sweep it along.

Suddenly, right in the middle of the channel, the water became even rougher. The water was whirling around in a circular motion and was foaming white. It was a whirlpool! The water was probably churning around a log or a big stone stuck on the bottom of the river. If the whirlpool pulled Tomero toward its center, he could be sucked down and drowned. Tomero knew he would have to get out of the channel and move closer to the shore, even though that, too, would be dangerous.

Tomero steered desperately toward the side of the river. Once he was downstream from the whirlpool, he paddled back to the safety of the middle of the river. He sighed with relief as he left the roaring "demon" behind him. The last time he had passed there, the water had been slightly bubbling. Now he realized why—the whirlpool had been forming even then.

Below the whirlpool, Tomero passed lands which the

river was flooding. Cottonwood and willow trees stood in water three feet deep, but the dense willow roots kept the land from completely washing away. Behind the willows grew a forest of sycamore, elm, and ash. These great trees, some as big as twelve feet across, were laced together by drooping vines. The underbrush was thick, pierced only by Indian trails, a foot wide.

As the canoe bounced on the current, Tomero saw a puma moving among the willows. Such a great cat wasn't frightening to him. He was used to hunting buffalo. Now he needed the puma for food because he was many miles from the nearest village where he could get something to eat.

Tomero never worried about finding food on the river. From his canoe he could shoot fish with his bow and arrow. Ashore he hunted bears, elk, raccoons, opossums, and squirrels. He could always find roots to eat, maybe a few berries and leaves. Water to drink was never a problem. All he had to do was dip his paddle into the river, hold it up at an angle, and water would run off into his mouth. Now, tonight, puma would make a good meal.

Tomero paddled ashore. Following the puma's tracks along the muddy shoreline was easy. Within minutes, the animal was dead, a spear thrust into its side.

Gathering some dry moss, Tomero placed a small pile on a piece of dry wood. Then from his supplies, he took his bow and arrow. Pressing the upright arrow into a groove in the wood, he twisted the bowstring around the arrow. Vigorously, he moved his bow back and forth which twirled the arrow very fast causing the wood to get hot. The heat from the rubbing lit the moss. Soon the flames were roasting chunks of puma meat. Tomero bit a hunk of meat and swallowed it.

Nearby several black vultures were perched, waiting, watching him, hissing. They had smelled the meat and flown down, expecting to gorge themselves on the dead puma. Tomero stared at the hungry birds. They stared back, unblinking, and watched him pop a piece of maple sugar candy into his mouth.

Tomero always packed candy in his canoe because he liked sweets. The women in his tribe had made the candy by boiling maple sap until only the syrup remained. They strained it through hemlock branches to remove any dirt. Then they cooled the syrup on the snow where it hardened into candy. It tasted good mixed with the flavor of puma meat.

The vultures moved closed. Thinking that the birds might claw him in order to get the meat, Tomero dragged the remains of the puma a short distance away from his camp. They attacked the cat, fighting for its flesh, tugging at the meat, devouring it. And they left Tomero alone.

That evening the moon rose, scattering light behind the willows. The river caught the light and sparkled silver. Tomero looked across the water and saw a shadow move. From the willows, a white-tailed deer stepped out to drink. Tomero crouched motionless, watching.

Nearby a black and white tail rose, wiggling, as a skunk scurried about digging for beetles in the mud. Its tail was dripping wet. Tomero's people used skunk skin for clothing. He watched the animal until it disappeared. Then he curled up beside the campfire with his feet toward the blaze for warmth.

Tomero watched a deer wade into the flooded Mississippi. (Illinois State Historical Library)

Tomero did not know that his camping ground was near an ancient waterfall over which the river had plunged millions of years ago. The waterfall had been worn away by the river's waters until the area became a narrow valley.

But the river began to chew that away, too. Year after year, it widened the valley by tearing away bits of the valley sides. With every spring flood, like the one in 1498, the river would overflow in some places. In other places, it would tear away pieces of land from the outer curves of the river bends, and pick up millions of tons of silt and sand.

All of this material was dropped either at the mouth of the river or at places where the current slowed down, such as at the inner curves of the river bends. The dropping of silt, sand, and gravel at the bends formed flat land areas, called floodplains, on both sides of the river. And when the river overflowed, it filled up the whole floodplain.

Sounds of a new day came to Tomero. The song of a red bird awoke him. The cardinal was always the first song bird to sing in the morning and the last one to sing at dusk.

Tomero opened his eyes to see that the river had disappeared! During the night, the evil spirits had breathed a thick white smoke over the water. Terrified, Tomero raised his head in prayer to the Great Spirit. Actually the river's disappearance was caused by a fog. Finally, it lifted and the river lay before Tomero, looking gray and smelling of willows. He continued his journey. The river was lower now—the floodwater had gone down a little during the night.

Many days later, evil spirits again came upon "Father of Waters," filling the whole river with an eerie silence. Tomero turned his canoe for shore. But before he could reach its safety, a powerful wind struck. The canoe overturned, and Tomero plunged into the water, dark and deep.

Quickly, he swam upward. Bursting into the air, he threw his arms about the overturned canoe and hauled himself onto the craft. It almost righted itself.

Great waves washed over Tomero. Rain beat down and

hid the shoreline. Struggling and sputtering, he clung to the canoe and managed to hold on. The heaving waves tossed the canoe downstream, lifting Tomero, driving him down, and then finally slamming the canoe against the bank.

Tomero's feet sank into mud. He yanked them out, crawled over the canoe, and stood on solid ground. Facing the slashing rain and wind, he pulled the craft from the water. The canoe lay upside down, its willow frame still in good shape. Exhausted, Tomero crawled under it and hid from the storm.

The rain passed as quickly as it had come. But the wind continued, leaving the river ruffled white with waves. Tomero knew it would be sometime before the river would calm itself and welcome him again. So he camped along the shore for a few days.

Tomero unpacked his canoe and discovered that all of his candy and some of his supplies were gone. He grunted in disgust. From the Choctaw he could obtain new supplies, but not candy. He dried out the animal skins in which the pipestones were wrapped. Fortunately, they had been stored under another skin which had been fastened to the sides of the canoe. It had kept the pipestones from being lost in the storm.

In three days, Tomero packed his canoe and set off again. Beneath him, the river was hardly moving. Suddenly, a gigantic catfish swam alongside the canoe, its gray head above the waters. Sent by the Great Spirit, the creature had come to celebrate the canoe's safe delivery from the storm. Tomero spoke gently to the fish.

"I knew you were watching me. I am ashamed to say that I was afraid. But now that you have come, I know the rest of my journey will be safe."

The fish rolled on its side and disappeared into the depths of the river. Tomero raised his head in joyful thanks to the Great Spirit.

As the catfish had foretold, Tomero arrived safely at the lowest part of the Mississippi. His business with the Choctaw was successful. The pipestones were exchanged for the most beautiful pink conch shells he had ever seen. He could almost hear the joyful cries of the men and women in his village.

Having completed his trading, Tomero decided to relax and enjoy himself. He paddled to the mouth of the great river where he saw the Mississippi disappear into the sea. The ocean waves were enormous, thunderous, full of power. He clung to the sides of the canoe and let it roll with the surf. His laughs of delight filled the air.

Then out in the ocean, gliding past him like a monster, sailed a canoe more massive than he had ever imagined. It was crowned with great pieces of white cloth. Tomero sat in wonder watching until it disappeared, far out at sea.

Tomero never knew that the great canoe was a Spanish ship called *El Correo,* "The Mail." It was sailed by some of Christopher Columbus's men, the first European explorers to see the mouth of the Mississippi. Tomero turned his canoe into the river's sprawling opening.

The following day, he began his journey up the Mississippi. His muscles bulged and his body sweated as he fought to paddle against the current. Tomero stayed close to the shoreline, for it was only here that the waves pushed his canoe a little upstream.

But he paddled with joy, for he knew that his journey would be safe. The great fish had told him so. And he paddled with pride, for he knew how pleased his village people would be with his trade. His canoe carried the beautiful conch shells.

2

Journey of the French Explorers 1673

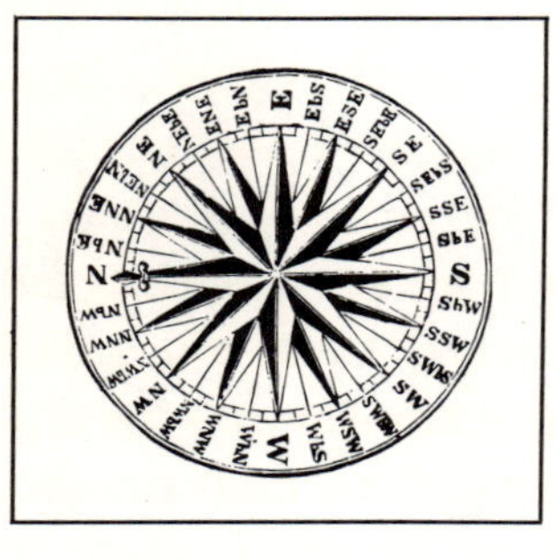

For the next 43 years, the Indians had the Mississippi River to themselves. Then it became known to European explorers.

A Spaniard named Hernando de Soto claimed the Mississippi for the king of Spain in 1541. He called it "Rio Grande," meaning "grand" or "big" river. But the Spanish later gave the name "Rio Grande" to the river which flows along the Texas-Mexico border.

The Spanish were the first Europeans to open North America to colonization, claiming land in the southern and southeastern parts of the continent (what is now Mexico and

Florida). Soon, France, England, the Netherlands, and Portugal had settlements in North America.

As England expanded its colonies along the Atlantic coast, France was determined to gain control of northern and central North America. For years, French explorers had heard Indians talk about a wide, muddy river called the *Mesipi,* the Ojibway Indian word meaning "big river."

Were the Mesipi and Rio Grande the same river? The French government wanted to know. If one river flowed through the heart of North America, France wanted to claim it. Possibly forts could be built along its banks to protect the French from English attack. Indians might be persuaded to trade their fur pelts, or skins, for French goods. And if there were mines of silver, copper, lead, and gold, they would enrich the treasury of the French King. Finally, the river might be a way to get behind the English colonies, and drive them out of the continent.

Fortunately, France had just the man for gathering information about the Mississippi. He was 29-year-old Louis Jolliet who had already worked for the government as a spy and explorer. Jolliet was a surveyor and an excellent map drawer. Because his main business was fur trading, he knew people in several Indian tribes and spoke their languages.

On a May morning in 1673, Jolliet and his men loaded supplies into two birch canoes. The 20-foot crafts easily held bags of dried corn, smoked meat, muskets, and canvas sails for making the canoes move faster.

Five of the six men with Jolliet were *voyageurs,* professional rivermen, who worked for fur trading companies. Traveling the rivers in their canoes, they moved furs between remote wilderness places. They were strong, bold Frenchmen, but very superstitious.

They believed the Indian stories about the monsters, the deadly heat, and the whirlpools that were said to be along the river. To their minds, monsters were real and terrible creatures. But, to Jolliet, such creatures existed only in Indian tales.

The sixth man was Jacques Marquette, a Catholic priest of the Society of Jesus, or the Jesuit Order. Marquette planned to establish a church mission among the Indians of the Mississippi Valley. He wore a long black robe and cape, and a cross hung around his neck, under the cape. Years before, an Iliniwek Indian had come to the priest's Wisconsin mission and told of his home along the Mississippi. Marquette was determined to find these Indians and preach to them.

When the last bag of corn was stored in the canoes, the Frenchmen set off from Michilimackinac, Michigan. For nearly a month they traveled southwest, across Lake Michigan, making their way into Lake Winnebago, and then on to the lower Fox. They paddled on the lower Fox until they reached the head of that river, and could go no farther by water.

The explorers then carried their canoes and supplies through a forest until they reached another river, the Wisconsin. They followed this river for one week, until it emptied into a much wider river.

"This must be the Mississippi!" Jolliet shouted to Marquette. "It flows south and looks almost a mile wide."

Marquette agreed. As the river swept his canoe downstream, he made notes about the region in his journal.

In the other canoe, Jolliet drew a map. He sketched in the high distant hills along the western bank and the islands which divided the river in many places. One voyageur used a piece of lead fastened to a long line to discover that the water depth in some places was 114 feet! Jolliet recorded this information in his journal and dated it: June 17, 1673.

Suddenly, a catfish slammed into Jolliet's canoe, bending the boat's thin ribs. He had never seen such a fish! Jolliet peered into the clear water, looking for more gigantic creatures, but there were none.

At dusk, Jolliet ordered his men ashore to prepare the evening meal. Standing on the bank, the voyageurs threw a net into the darkening water and caught a green fish which had a paddle-shaped snout. But they would not eat the strange looking fish, even though Jolliet tried to convince them it looked tasty.

He and Marquette ate the green fish which was actually a Mississippi paddlefish. Though rare today, it was plentiful in those days. Meanwhile, the voyageurs caught and devoured a sturgeon, a fish they had often eaten.

Jolliet had anchored the canoes offshore, opposite a high bluff. "It's safer for us to sleep aboard," he explained, "while one man stays on watch for Indians and river creatures."

The third day on the Mississippi, Jolliet noticed that the hills were becoming smaller, and the land was often flat and covered with grass. Ashore, he hunted buffalo and wild turkeys.

Marquette, meanwhile, looked in vain for Indians. Finally, on June 25, he saw footprints in the muddy river bank which led to a trail. Marquette and Jolliet followed the path, while the voyageurs stayed with the canoes.

About five miles inland, they found three Indian villages along a river. This river is believed to be either the Des Moines or Iowa, in what is now the state of Iowa.

Approaching the closest village, the explorers shouted. Instantly, Indians came running from all directions. Four moved toward Jolliet and Marquette. Two carried red tobacco pipes trimmed with feathers. They came slowly, raising their pipes toward the sun. Their naked bodies were covered with tattoos.

Hoping these Indians were Iliniwek, Marquette asked them who they were in the Iliniwek language.

Surprise shone on their faces. "We are Iliniwek," they replied, "a tribe of Peoria." They held their pipes for the Frenchmen to smoke.

Marquette was delighted to have found the Indians. He and Jolliet puffed on the pipes. They knew that smoking symbolized peace to these Indians who worshipped the sun. But why? They didn't understand. They only knew that whenever the Indians wanted rain or other weather changes, they would raise their pipes to the sun.

When the explorers finished smoking, they entered the village where they met the great Captain, or Chief. Standing naked in the doorway of his hut, the Chief held his pipe for the men to smoke. He then honored them by having them sit on a mat inside his hut and having their feet rubbed with bear grease.

The Frenchmen explained their voyage.

This artist's drawing shows Jolliet and Marquette meeting the Peoria Indians. Marquette holds the peace calumet. Descendants of the Peoria now live in Oklahoma. (Illinois State Historical Library)

Impressed because they had come such a long way to visit him, the Chief gave them his ten-year-old son, White Owl.

Jolliet turned to Marquette and spoke in French. "This boy is probably a slave, captured from another tribe. Do you wish to be responsible for him?"

"No," answered Marquette softly. "We have no choice but to take him with us. We cannot offend the Chief. Let us be grateful now, for he is giving us his pipe. He values that more than the boy."

Jolliet thanked the Chief as he accepted the pipe. It was a peace calumet, a symbol of peace. If the pipe were a war calumet, it would be decorated with red feathers.

According to custom, the Chief ordered a meal for the visitors. Women entered the hut, carrying platters filled with corn, fish, and buffalo meat. Kneeling before the Frenchmen, they placed the food on their tongues. One woman dangled dog meat before Jolliet. He refused to eat it. Dog meat was a delicacy among these people. Sometimes the Indians hoisted dogs to the tops of poles as sacrifices to the spirits, especially in times of great happiness or sadness.

The Chief allowed the explorers to wander through his village. An orator ran ahead of them, shouting for everyone to come out to see the white-skinned men. Some people lay on the grass staring at them. A women gave them belts made of buffalo hair. To their horror, they saw that she didn't have any ears or a nose.

"Her husband has cut them off because she has been unfaithful to him," explained the orator. "Sometimes a man scalps his wife for being disloyal."

The next day Jolliet and Marquette returned to their canoes, followed by 600 Indians, the Chief, and White Owl. Jolliet put the boy in his canoe and the explorers left.

Two hundred miles down the Mississippi, the men faced another terrible sight. Two monsters painted on a white rock wall glared at them. White Owl crouched on the floor of the canoe, terrified. Marquette wrote in his journal that "each had

The cliff on which the monsters appeared is gone, blasted away for its limestone. The Piasa, repainted on another cliff behind a gasoline station, is barely visible at Alton, Illinois. (Illinois State Historical Library)

horns and the face of a bearded man. The body was covered with scales and ended with a long, winding tail."

The creature was actually the Piasa (an Indian word meaning "man-devouring-bird"). It was supposed to have eaten people and been killed by Indians with poisoned arrows.

The explorers were so busy discussing the paintings, no one noticed that the river was moving swifter. Suddenly a rapid current caught the canoes. The men pulled away just as trees and a great swell of yellow water rushed into the Mississippi. White Owl explained that it was the mouth of the Pekitanoui, its waters pouring into the Mississippi.

The river was called by its Indian name, meaning "muddy water," until 1712. Then it was named the Missouri.

Farther south, the canoes passed the Kaskaskia River,

near Tomero's village, which had disappeared. Indians of the seventeenth century knew nothing about it. There was no written record of its existence, and all the stories about the village had been forgotten.

Two days later, they came to the mouth of another wide river.

"It is the Ohio!" White Owl exclaimed. "The beautiful river."

Jolliet smiled at White Owl. The boy's unexpected knowledge of the river was proving helpful. He was intelligent and eager to learn. Jolliet was teaching him French.

Beyond the Ohio River, the grass grew so thick and high that even the buffalo could hardly walk through it. Jolliet now knew he was on the same river which de Soto had discovered. He was experiencing what the Spaniard had reported.

The river, snaking its way through vast green swamps, was hardly moving. The sun was unbelievably hot and the mosquitoes hovered in thick clouds over the water. The explorers kept slapping themselves and wiping sweat off their skin. Their clothes clung to the body. Hot and miserable, they reached a Chickasaw village.

The Chickasaw allowed them to rest in the cool shade of a hut. While relaxing, they watched an Indian tattoing himself. Stretching his skin, he pricked out a design with a sharp fishbone, and rubbed charcoal into the punctures.

The explorers could easily talk with the Chickasaw because their language was known to the Iliniwek and White Owl. Chickasaw was a language of trade throughout the lower

Mississippi Valley. The Chickasaw people assured Jolliet that the explorers were close to the mouth of the river.

The journey continued. But as the men approached another settlement, they became alarmed. Along the bank stood Indians with spears, bows, hatchets, and clubs. As a spear pierced Jolliet's canoe, he raised his musket.

Marquette held up the peace calumet which the Peoria Captain had given them. The Indians paid no attention to it! One hurled his club at the priest.

Suddenly, two older Indians saw the peace calumet and ordered the attack stopped. Jolliet and his companions were welcomed ashore. Although the Indians were of the Quapaw tribe, one man who spoke a little Iliniwek explained that his own people were Michigamea, an Iliniwek tribe. However, the group had moved south long ago and developed its own dialect. Its people no longer understood the Iliniwek language.

The Indians guided the Frenchmen farther south, down the Mississippi, to the mouth of what is now the Arkansas River. When they came upon a village of Arkansas Indians, Jolliet didn't like what he saw. The Arkansas carried Spanish guns. Now he knew that the Spaniards had come this far north. Surely, the Mississippi flowed through land which Spain claimed and on to the Gulf of Mexico. Since the Spaniards would never permit the Frenchmen to explore their land, Jolliet decided to return north, back up the Mississippi.

But they didn't leave quickly enough. Already some Arkansas Indians had decided to kill the explorers. However, the Chief discovered the plan and ordered it stopped.

Michigamea Indians guided the explorers down the twisting waterways of the Mississippi. Today, much of the course down which Jolliet and Marquette paddled is solid ground. (Illinois State Historical Library)

Traveling north, against the strong current, was hard work. At last, they passed the Ohio and Missouri again, reaching the Illinois River where an Iliniwek tribe welcomed them. A brave guided them up to the head of that river and then overland to the lake of the Iliniwek (Lake Michigan). By going this way they did not have to travel back up the Wisconsin and Fox rivers.

Marquette had often been in poor health, and on the

return trip, he fell ill from dysentery. He was so sick that he was forced to remain in Green Bay, Wisconsin. When he recovered, he returned to his mission and wrote about his Mississippi voyage. He died in 1675.

Jolliet was full of new energy after his Mississippi adventure. He had become fond of White Owl and had exciting plans for him. He wanted to take the boy to Canada and enroll him in a school.

On the way, Jolliet tried to navigate through the dangerous Lachine Rapids of the St. Lawrence River. The rushing waters slammed his canoe against a rock, shattering the craft to pieces. White Owl and two voyageurs drowned. Jolliet lost all his records about the Mississippi. Fishermen who had seen the accident pulled him from the water.

Jolliet drew another map of the river from memory, and described his experiences to the French government.

"Most Indians are friendly," he reported. "France can enjoy a good trading business with them. Forts can be built along the banks. But there is no gold to be found, only a long, winding trade route."

When Jolliet died in 1700, 27 years after his voyage, most of the Indians along the Mississippi were killing beavers, deer, and buffalo, and selling the pelts to the French. However, a few tribes, like the powerful Chickasaw, sided with the English in their war, soon to be fought with the French, over possession of the Mississippi Valley.

3

A Boy Builds on the Mississippi

1764

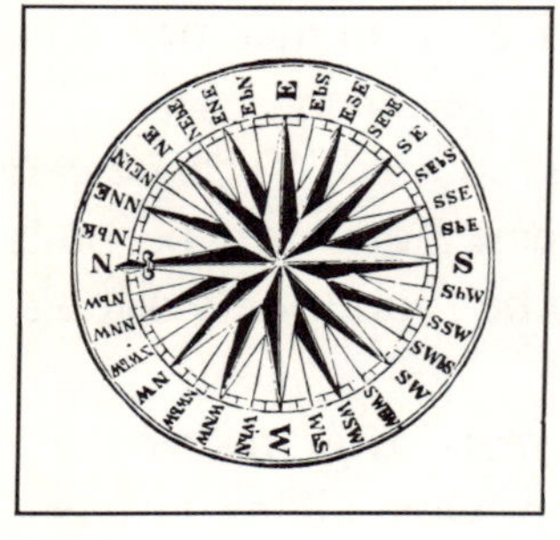

France soon discovered that Spain wasn't interested in the Mississippi. Spaniards were finding gold and silver in Mexico and South America. Therefore, when French explorer Robert La Salle journeyed down the river in 1682, he claimed the entire Mississippi Valley for France. He named the land Louisiana in honor of his king, Louis XIV.

In those days, no one knew where the Mississippi began, nor over how large an area the river flowed. But gradually, the Mississippi Valley came to mean to the French all the land drained by the Mississippi, Missouri, Ohio, and Arkansas rivers.

Louis XIV sent Frenchmen to build settlements along the river. In 1686, one of La Salle's men, Henri de Tonti, established a fur trading post and village at the mouth of the Arkansas River, near the spot where Jolliet had met and stayed a few days with the Quapaw people. Tonti called the settlement Arkansas Post.

About 200 miles south of Arkansas Post, and only 110 miles north of the river's mouth on the Gulf of Mexico, other colonists built log huts and called their village La Nouvelle-Orleans in honor of the king's younger brother, the Duke of Orleans.

But here the river was much wider, the plants and animals were different, and the Indians were more dangerous than anywhere else in the valley. The land was so swampy that the streets sank and became ditches. The ditches filled up with mosquitoes and alligators which attacked the colonists, giving them malaria or painful wounds which wouldn't heal.

Still, the Frenchmen kept building. They brought black slaves from Africa to drain the swamps, chop down trees, and build an embankment to keep out the Mississippi.

Then, in 1759, the English drove the French out of the Mississippi Valley east of the river. The vast, unknown land west of the river and the area around New Orleans remained under French control. Or so people thought.

Actually, Louis XV—the new king of France—had given away everything, including the town and district around it, to his cousin, Charles III, king of Spain. Louis didn't tell his subjects about the gift for two years, so naturally everyone thought that New Orleans and the land west of the river still belonged to the French.

One such person was 13-year-old Rene Auguste Chouteau, called Auguste. His stepfather, Pierre Laclede, had recently obtained a license from the French government to trade with the Indians of the Mississippi Valley. The license gave Pierre the right to build on the Mississippi's west bank. Because Auguste was a good worker, honest, and respected by adults, Pierre put him in charge of building the trading post and village.

Auguste left his New Orleans home in 1763, and came with his stepfather to Fort de Chartres, situated on the Mississippi in what is now Illinois, and about 25 miles south of the present city of St. Louis. This settlement was the only protected place in the midwest large enough to house all the equipment and men needed for building the trading post and village.

From the fort, Auguste and Pierre traveled by boat up the twisting Mississippi River to look for a good place to build the post. Pierre steered close to the bank where the big roots of trees, like snakes, crawled out from the earth. On the eastern side, they passed low swamplands filled with cottonwood and cypress trees. But on the west side, tall, yellow bluffs arose.

In the sky, their attention was held by a moving dark line. Auguste and Pierre watched as the line grew longer until the sky was filled with flocks of birds. At first, Auguste thought they were ducks. But as they came closer, beating the air with their white wings, he saw they were trumpeter swans. Thousands of them flew over his head. Auguste had never seen anything so

Cypress swamps lay dark and quiet along the Illinois shoreline. Such swamps are common today along the southern parts of the river. (Illinois State Historical Library)

beautiful. The great birds swooped in the air and settled down upon a sandbar which ran out into the river.

The boat continued upstream. Auguste looked back to see the swans treading in the shallow water. They lowered their long necks, reached into the water with their black bills, and pulled up plants from the river bottom.

That evening, as the sun sank below the horizon and the sky glowed a brilliant pink, Auguste and Pierre found the land they had been seeking. It was a central location, within 100 miles of the mouths of several great rivers—the Missouri, Ohio, and Illinois. They all flowed into the Mississippi and all wer[illegible] trading routes.

From the boat, Pierre and Auguste looked up to a hig[illegible] slope. "It is perfect!" exclaimed Pierre. "And not part of th[illegible] floodplain."

"What do you mean?" asked Auguste.

"It is not flat land made by the river. The land atop that slope is high enough to keep the river from washing away our trading post and village.

"Yes. It is perfect," Pierre repeated. He beached the boat for the night.

Pierre wasn't disappointed the next day. Not only was the land a good location, it was beautiful. He and Auguste roamed along a sparkling stream which quickly branched off into a creek, and then into a river. They explored the woods where deer, bears, raccoons, and beavers lived.

Pierre cut out pieces of bark from some trees to mark the place for the trading post so Auguste could find it later. Winter was coming so Auguste couldn't begin building until spring. Meanwhile, they would plan and map out their project back at the fort.

Fort de Chartres fascinated Auguste. Of all the forts ever built in North America it was the best constructed. Its gray stone walls, 15 feet high, three feet thick, and 490 feet long, surrounded several buildings which were made of limestone and

Fort de Chartres stood alongside the Mississippi. Today, only one of the original buildings remains. The fort, now being restored, is an Illinois State Park. (Illinois State Historical Library)

timber. Limestone had been found in hills close to the fort, and timber had been cut from the nearby forest.

Built by the French, the fort was a government headquarters for settlers and fur traders of the Mississippi Valley. French soldiers stationed there protected passing flatboats from robbers. The flatboats brought bags of peppers, buttons, boots, fishhooks, and other items to trading posts along the river. One such store was inside the fort.

A soldier told Auguste that the fort was in danger of falling into the river. Auguste could see that it was. A sandbar which had formed along the opposite bank had caused the Mississippi to swing from its course and wash against the shoreline near the fort.

"People used to wade across the river to the sandbar," said the soldier. "But now the water on this side is 40 feet deep."

"Why did the French build so close to the river?" Auguste asked.

"They didn't!" exclaimed the soldier. "When this stone fort was begun in 1753, the Mississippi was one and one-half miles away. Nine years later, it was within half a mile of the fort. Now it is about 26 yards and still coming closer."

"How are you people going to protect the fort?"

"Have you forgotten that since the war this land now belongs to England?" the soldier asked, surprised. "Every day we expect English troops to come and take over the fort."

All winter, Auguste looked for the soldiers to arrive. They still hadn't come by the time he and 30 workmen left the settlement in February of 1764 and went up river. They traveled by flatboat until Auguste saw the cut-marked trunks. He ordered the boat to land and directed the men to set up camp. Supplies and tools were unloaded.

The next morning, Auguste seized an axe, approached a tree, and chopped it down. The building of what was to be St. Louis, Missouri, was begun! Auguste had just turned fourteen.

In April, Pierre came to inspect the work. Auguste showed him a toolshed and several cabins which had been built. Pierre was pleased. He gave Auguste his final plans for the village and his own house. Then Pierre returned to the fort. He was anxious to remove the last of his supplies before the English came.

No sooner had Pierre left, then Auguste was faced with a problem—Indians. A large group of them arrived at the building site.

With only 30 men to back him, Auguste stood before 150 warriors and several women and children. He didn't know what to expect. The little he knew about Indians was based on what Pierre had told him about trading with them.

The warriors explained in broken French that they were a Missouri tribe. Poor and hungry, they were looking for new land on which to settle. The land around the house which Auguste was building looked good to them. They decided they wanted to build their village there.

Alarmed, Auguste tried to talk the warriors out of this idea. One Indian shook a club in his face. Another raised his rifle. They set up camp, prepared to stay. Auguste sent a workman to bring Pierre back.

While waiting for his stepfather, Auguste thought of a way to make the Indians leave. He remembered that Pierre had told him that in almost all Indian tribes, the men considered most work something for the women to do. He thought that if he ordered the Indians to work, they would leave. He directed them to dig out the cellar for Pierre's house. The women and children obeyed. For two weeks, they carried out dirt in wooden platters and in baskets on their heads.

Auguste finished building his stepfather's house in 1765. Laclède's house was the first family dwelling built in St. Louis. (Missouri Historical Society)

But the warriors refused to work. "Carrying dirt is women's work," they told Auguste. "We are warriors, not beasts of burden. We risk our lives to fight enemy tribes and kill game. When we kill an animal, we leave the creature where it fell, and mark a trail from it back to our camp. Our women follow the trail and carry back the carcass. We do not carry carcasses. We will not carry dirt!"

Auguste didn't know how to reason with them.

Some took tools, explaining that they weren't really stealing. Instead, they were playing a game. Auguste didn't understand such games. He was fast becoming desperate. How he wished Pierre were here!

Finally, his stepfather arrived. But he couldn't persuade the Indians to leave, either. At last, he alarmed them with news that 600 warriors who had waged war against them were gathered at Fort de Chartres.

"If these Indians learn you are here," Pierre warned, "they will come here to kill you and make slaves of your women and children."

Frightened by the news, the Indians left the next day and returned to their village along the Missouri River.

Before long, Auguste and Pierre learned that their new village was on Spanish land. Auguste was upset, but not as much as Pierre. The older man was furious! Never once had he imagined that he had chosen Spanish land for his French village. He had even named it St. Louis in honor of Louis IX, the crusader king of France. All its people, their language, customs, manners, and laws were to be French. And all the time his French village had been Spanish? He couldn't believe it!

Fortunately, Spain sent Pedro de Piernas to govern St. Louis. Piernas was a quiet and gentle man. Married to a French woman, he quickly won Pierre's friendship.

Then, in 1778, Pierre died during a voyage on the Mississippi. Auguste was sick with grief as he took over his stepfather's trading business. Following Pierre's example, Auguste treated the Indians fairly. Because he was so honest in his dealings with them, the Indians said, "If a Chouteau word, it was fact."

Auguste's business was thriving when the American

Revolution ended in 1783. Seven years earlier, 13 of Britain's North American colonies revolted and united to form a single government—the United States. The American Revolution had begun. In 1778, Colonel George Rogers Clark led an American invasion of the Mississippi Valley. In less than a year, he succeeded in driving out the British.

In 1792, revolutionists took over the French government, and royalty ended. Napoleon Bonaparte, a dictator, gained control of the country. He managed to get Louisiana returned to France.

Then, in 1803, Napoleon sold the Louisiana Territory to the United States. The purchase doubled the land area of the country. Now the entire Mississippi Valley belonged to the United States.

Auguste watched pioneers arrive in St. Louis. They purchased supplies from his trading post, and then boarded steamboats which took them 400 miles up the Missouri River, to the bend at the Kansas border. Here, where the Missouri River swings north, the frontier towns of Independence, Westport Landing (the future Kansas City), and St. Joseph were built. Thousands of covered wagons and people were moved by steamers from St. Louis to these three frontier towns. From these settlements, wagons rolled westward to Oregon and California. St. Louis, mushrooming into a city along the river, became known as the "Gateway to the West."

Auguste was amazed. As a boy building a village, he never once thought of starting a city. But he had! He was called "The First American Citizen of the Mississippi Valley." It was a title of which he was very proud. He died in 1829.

4

Abraham Lincoln's Journey 1831

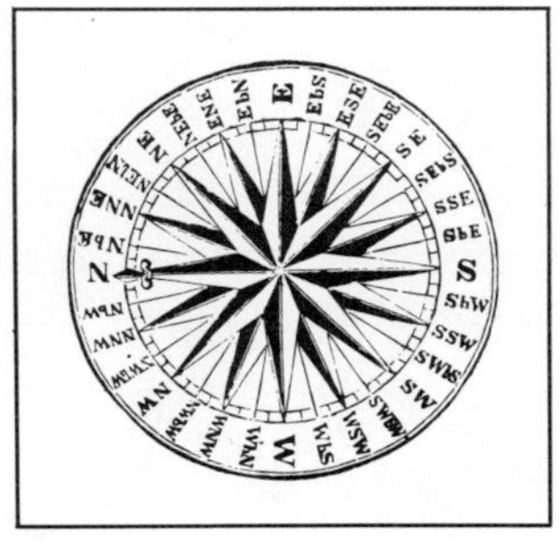

President Thomas Jefferson's purchase of Louisiana opened the entire Mississippi River as a trade route to Europe, Latin America, and western North America. Midwest farmers loaded their goods on flatboats and floated down the Mississippi to New Orleans. Merchants bought the produce for sale there or shipment overseas.

Foreign ships, their hulls filled with English china, expensive linen and silk fabrics from Europe, tropical fruits from Central America, and African cocoa beans, docked at the waterfront. Businessmen bought these goods and sold them in New Orleans. Sometimes, the goods were placed on steamboats and shipped north for sale.

Moving down the Mississippi on a flatboat in the spring of 1831 was twenty-two-year-old Abraham Lincoln. He was working for Denton Offutt, a merchant from New Salem, Illinois. Offutt had hired Abe, his step-brother John D. Johnston, and his cousin John Hanks to build a flatboat, load it with merchandise, and take the goods to New Orleans for sale there. Offutt was paying each of them $12 a month.

For six weeks, the men had worked on the boat and camped in a hut at Sangamo Town along the Sangamon River in central Illinois. They sawed planks from tree logs and pegged them together to make a raft-like boat, 80 feet long and 18 feet wide. It had plank sides, a flat bottom and it was square at both ends. In the middle of the boat, they built a cabin and pen to hold barrels of flour and cornmeal, casks of salt pork, and thirty

Steamboats and flatboats crowded the Mississippi River as Abe piloted his boat downriver in 1831. (Illinois State Historical Library)

squealing hogs. Once the boat was loaded, they had gone with Offutt down the Sangamon River to the Illinois, and then into the Mississippi.

As the flatboat slid around a river bend, Abe's eyes looked ahead to search for fallen trees in the water. He spied one and steered around it. For steering, he used a large oar made of a long pole with a square plank tied at one end as a "paddle."

A snag—tree hidden under the water—could wreck a flatboat. Abe had learned about snags three years before, when he had taken a cargo of goods to New Orleans. He had been a hired hand then. Now he was the captain and pilot. His job was to steer safely to New Orleans.

Abe's first stop on the Mississippi was at St. Louis where dozens of steamers and hundreds of flatboats lined the wharves. He pulled in long enough to let off John Hanks who wanted to return to his family in Illinois. Then Abe continued south, steering clear of the steamboats and their whitewater wakes. The fast-moving steamers sometimes crashed into the slow-moving flatboats.

Abe thought that any boat which moved upstream against the current was a miracle. Three decks high, the steamboats were loaded with passengers, furniture, clothing, lumber, and food. Abe watched clouds of smoke pour from the two big black smokestacks toward the front of a steamer. Below deck, where Abe couldn't see, wood was being cut and loaded into the ship's fiery furnace. The fire boiled water which created steam to make the ship's paddle wheel turn and move the boat.

Downstream, Abe floated past New Madrid, Missouri.

Looking up at the town, he asked Offutt about the earthquakes that had occurred there twenty years ago.

"I heard tell," recalled Abe, "that the river banks caved in and part of New Madrid fell into the river."

"Weren't only there," claimed Offutt. "Them banks fell in as far away as Vicksburg, Mississippi, and made Reelfoot Lake in Tennessee."

Offutt had told Abe correctly. But he didn't realize how terrible the quakes of 1811 and 1812 had been. Shocks were felt from Canada to New Orleans, and from the headwaters of the Missouri River in Montana, to the Atlantic Ocean.

Waves on the Mississippi had started at different places and then met, crashing together in violent blows. The earth beneath the river cracked. Water turned upstream. Many people thought that the Mississippi had swung back on itself and was running backwards. The course of the river changed as banks collapsed and water tore through grasslands and forests.

Near New Madrid, where the quakes were centered, great clouds of dust arose and blocked out the sunlight. Sand was all over the place. Cabins lay in broken heaps. Although New Madrid was destroyed, only one person was killed in the town.

Abe stared up at New Madrid, now completely rebuilt.

Farther downstream, he pulled into the waterfront of Memphis, Tennessee. Along the wharves were hundreds of Indians dressed in rags. These people were Creeks, Choctaws, Chickasaws, Cherokees, and Seminoles. The federal government wanted their lands for white settlers. It had paid them for their lands and then ordered them to move west of the Missis-

The earthquake at New Madrid. Cabins crumbled, trees waved together, and the ground sunk. Flashes of lightning gleamed through the dark clouds. (Missouri Historical Society)

sippi. Either the Indians moved, or the government would send troops to kill them.

From the flatboat, Abe watched an Indian family trudging along the waterfront and felt sorry for them.

A few days later, the flatboat entered the rough current above Vicksburg, Mississippi. In an instant, the rushing water whirled the boat close to the bank. On the shore near a log hut stood a man chopping down a tree. The wood would be used as

fuel for the furnace of a steamboat. The flatboat left the man far behind.

Abe tried to steer the boat, but the oar seemed to have no power. His arm felt completely numb. He turned the oar over to John. Between the two of them, they managed to hold onto the oar for sixty miles, all the way to Grand Gulf (near Vicksburg), Mississippi. From there to Natchez, Abe knew the river lay smooth. He and John relaxed while Offutt steered.

The old city of Natchez had two sections—the main town high up on bluffs overlooking the river, and the waterfront district which was known as Natchez-Under-the-Hill. And it was here that Abe tied up his flatboat for the night.

The streets of Natchez-Under-the Hill were walled with cotton bales, waiting to be moved by creaking wagons to flatboats and steamers at the dock. Abe noticed that Silver Street, the town's main road, was sliding into the river. The river will gnaw this town away, he thought.

The rough frontiersmen, riverboatmen, and riverboat traffic attracted gamblers, outlaws, and criminals. Natchez-Under-the-Hill was known as one of the most violent and lawless towns on the continent. The decent people of Natchez never went down to the waterfront except to take steamers or to trade.

Because it wasn't safe to leave the flatboat unguarded, Lincoln's crew took turns guarding the boat. But Abe never slept that night even though he was very tired. He remembered the last time he'd been near this place. Seven men had jumped his boat and beaten him up. Somehow he had managed to drive the men away. Abe lay awake all night. When morning came, the flatboat from Illinois was the first one to cast off.

South of Natchez, Abe's weary eyes gazed at the cotton and sugarcane fields which lay on either side of the river. He looked up to the silvery moss hanging from the black limbs of cypress trees. Along the shore he spotted a heron wading near a sleeping alligator.

From Baton Rouge, Louisiana, to New Orleans, the flatboat moved past grand plantations. Abe thought of slavery as he looked up the avenues of live oaks leading to the elegant houses which were surrounded by growing fields and slave quarters.

At New Orleans, the flatboats were lined up for almost a mile. Ships from European ports tied up at the pier. Steamboats blew and whistled, sending up steam. Cotton bales towered on the wharves.

The waterfront was so crowded that Abe spent nearly an hour looking for a place to land the boat. He found one alongside Jackson Square, across from St. Louis Cathedral. High up, Abe saw the church's three towers and its stained-glass windows.

Offutt searched the waterfront for a broker to buy his goods. He found one and sold him all his cargo, including the boat's planks. The market for Illinois timber was good. It was usual for a flatboat to be broken up and sold rather than trying to move it back upstream against the swift Mississippi current.

As soon as Offutt paid him, Abe took off alone. He was

Abe tied up the flatboat at the New Orleans waterfront. Behind him stood the St. Louis Cathedral and a government building. The building on the far left was the city jail. (Drawing by Lloyd Ostendorf)

anxious to see again this magnificent city. The architecture of New Orleans fascinated him. He was used to seeing wooden buildings, not structures of brick.

He roamed through the narrow streets and patios of the French Quarter. He walked in and out of shops and cafes, and stopped in a restaurant to eat one of his favorite foods, oysters. Everywhere he went there was music. It floated through the swinging doors of cafes. Musicians played in the streets and from the balconies of theaters.

Toward evening, Abe leaned against an iron gate and admired the ladies walking to an opera house where people were performing a play sung in Italian. The ladies wore towering wigs and enormous skirts, six feet across. The gentlemen escorting them carried canes and wore waistcoats that reached to their knees.

It was almost dark when Abe walked past a cemetery. All the burial vaults were above ground. People couldn't bury their dead in the earth in New Orleans because water lay ten inches below the surface.

The next day, Abe went with John and Offutt to the French Market where an unbelievable variety of fruits from the tropics was being sold. Abe bought seafood to eat, while John picked up a curved yellow fruit. He started to bite into it.

"Wait!" shouted Abe. "You must skin it first. Haven't you ever seen a banana?"

"No," admitted John. "I've never even heard the word."

Abe laughed.

Walking along, the men came to a slave auction. Kneeling on the platform was a young Negro girl crying. Above her stood a man selling her to a group of businessmen. The man reached for the girl's arm and yanked her to her feet.

"Be silent!" he ordered. The girl trembled as the man's fingers dug into her arm.

Abe clenched his fists in anger. "By God, boys!" he exclaimed, "let's get away from this. If I ever get a chance to hit this thing, I'll hit it hard."

Abe explored New Orleans for a month before he ran out of money. Joseph Artus, a steamboat captain, hired him to

Abe came across a slave auction in New Orleans. The experience of seeing a young woman sold into slavery caused him to form ideas against the selling of people as slaves. (Illinois State Historical Library)

work on the steamer *North America*. Abe cut wood and loaded it into the ship's fiery furnace. When the steamer docked at St. Louis, he crossed the Mississippi and hiked all the way to New Salem, Illinois, where he had a job operating Offutt's general stores and gristmill.

While living in New Salem, Abe decided that he wanted to become a lawyer. He borrowed law books from a friend and studied hard. On April 15, 1837, he rode into Springfield, Illinois, to begin his law practice. On that day, Abe had lived half his life. Twenty-eight years later, on April 15, 1865, he would die of an assassin's bullet in Washington, D.C.

The last twenty-eight years of Abe's life were his most successful. Twice he was elected President of the United States. On September 22, 1862, he signed the Emancipation Proclamation. This document freed those slaves who were still behind the Confederate lines, while the country was fighting the Civil War. For this reason, Abraham Lincoln was known as "The Great Emancipator."

5

Mark Twain's Last Journey 1882

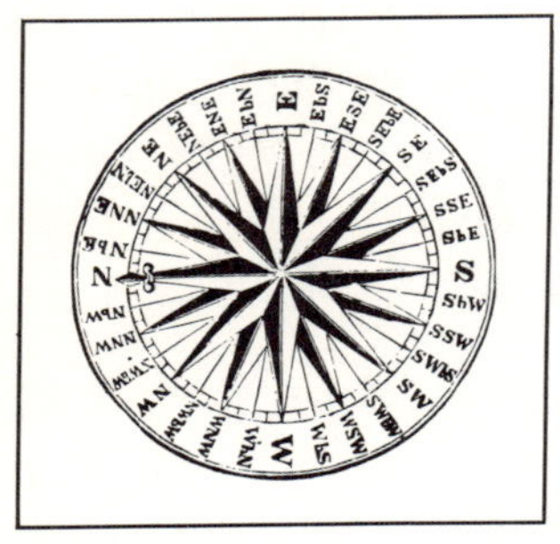

When the Civil War ended in 1865, railroads ran along the Mississippi River from north to south. As a result, steamboats lost business. They couldn't carry all the people and large amounts of freight the way a long train of cars could, pulled by one locomotive.

Steel wheels rolling on steel rails changed the appearance of the river. Tracks lined the banks, and bridges spanned the water so the railroads could get from one side of the Mississippi to the other. Sometimes steamboats crashed into bridge supports and sank. The first bridge to cross the river from Rock Island, Illinois, to Davenport, Iowa,

Men building the Illinois Central Railroad along the Mississippi River. (Illinois State Historical Library)

was built in 1855. It was nicknamed "Hellgate" by steamboat pilots.

One man who agreed with that description was Samuel L. Clemens. Out of the river had come his books —*Huckleberry Finn, The Adventures of Tom Sawyer,* and *Pudd'nhead Wilson.* Sam wrote these stories and many more under a name which forever linked him with the Mississippi —Mark Twain.

"Mark Twain" (twelve feet) was a river term which meant that a boat was floating just free of the bottom. Most

Mississippi River boats needed water 12 feet deep in order to float clear of the river bottom. Mark Twain was a name that suited Sam well, for he had met every character in his books on the river.

As a young man, Sam had piloted a Mississippi riverboat. Standing at the ship's wheel with a cigar between his teeth, dressed in a fancy suit, and wearing a gold watch chain, Sam was master over his steamboat. He loved the excitement of the river traffic, the busy waterfronts, the endless variety of people. Most of all, he loved the Mississippi.

Besides being a riverboat pilot, Sam had been a gold miner, a printer, and a journalist. Now at the age of 52, he was a famous author and still had more books to write. One book was *Life on the Mississippi*. As he began to write this book in his New England home, Sam felt a strong urge to return to the Mississippi and see again the sights he had loved as a boy. Thus, he came back to the river that he hadn't seen in 21 years.

In the spring of 1882, at St. Louis, Sam boarded a packet steamer, a boat that carries mail and cargo on a regular schedule. As the boat slid away from the pier, he looked back at twelve steamboats tied along the dock. They were not being used. Instead, trains were moving goods and people up and down the river. Sam felt very sad, for he remembered the days when he was a pilot and the steamers lined the St. Louis pier for a mile—all running and loaded with travelers and freight.

As Sam went down the Mississippi, he felt like the oldest man in the world. Everything was changed. He saw only one steamboat. Only one. She was sitting at rest in the shade within

Sam remembered what the St. Louis levee (landing) looked like in the old steamboat days when he was a riverboat captain. (Illinois State Historical Library)

the wooded mouth of a narrow river. Sam put his spy glass to his eye and smiled. The boat was named, "Mark Twain."

Many islands that Sam once knew had been in the river were no longer there. As the bends of the Mississippi had shifted from one side of the river to the other, the islands were either worn away or had become part of the riverbank. Wagons traveled where steamers used to navigate. Sam jotted down the names of the lost islands in his notebook.

He also noticed that the river had grown wider in places where trees had been cut for fifty yards on either side. The wood was used as fuel for steamers. Now the bare ground had caved into the river.

When darkness fell that first night, Sam shuddered. He

remembered how he used to search for his way in the blackness, trying to follow the deepest part of the channel so his boat could safely pass.

Wherever he could, Sam had used the white trunks of sycamore trees to guide him. All that was changed now. The federal government had turned the Mississippi into an avenue of lights. Along both sides of the river, the government set up oil lamps so the packets were never in the dark. A glowing lamp was either before or behind boats.

Sam shook his head sadly. Somehow the lamps took the excitement out of piloting. The danger of snags wasn't even there now. Government snag boats patrolled up and down the river, pulling up trees and brush. They allowed no new snags to collect either.

Sam soon discovered that the pilot of the packet had a new chartered river map, a lamp, and a compass. With a lamp by which to read the map, and with lights on the packet to find your way, a boat could run even in the fog. Unlike the old days, thought Sam. Now piloting was as safe and simple as driving a stagecoach.

Sam was happy to see that Osceola, Arkansas, looked as it had always looked by night, except for those lamps. He noticed a lot of light coming from the fleet of the United States River Commission along the shore.

The military engineers of the commission had decided to change the course of the Mississippi. They were building dams and digging channels to make the river flow where they had decided it should run. Their plans also included levees to protect the land from flooding, and hold the river to its course. For that purpose, they were chopping down trees along the banks so they could be covered with rocks. In many places, the shores were already lined with rocks, mounds of stone, or stone walls.

The project of controlling the river amused Sam. He knew that the Mississippi couldn't be controlled. He could almost hear the river laughing as it tore down dams and burst through stone walls. That river will flow where it wants, thought Sam.

Below Memphis, Tennessee, the river was pouring over the land and flooding the woods and fields for miles. Oil lamps stood in water three feet deep. The heavy spring rains had caused the river to rise.

Down in the black region of Arkansas and Mississippi, Sam saw poor people living along the river. Most of them stayed on the plantations. When they wanted to leave, they waved their arms for a packet to stop, and for $50 rode downstream to New Orleans, or upstream to St. Louis. Frequently, traveling families stopped the packet which Sam was riding. They carried what little they owned onto the boat, and hoped for a better life elsewhere.

For miles and miles, the packet passed cabins filled with Blacks. Cows stood around some cabins. Sam couldn't believe how bony the animals were. They resembled skeletons. Their only foods were bark and leaves. Grass didn't grow in this flood-wasted land.

Sam was disappointed to learn that the packet couldn't steam past Vicksburg, Mississippi. The river had cut across a loop above the city, and had left Vicksburg by itself on an old, winding curve. The river bend, now completely surrounded by land, was an oxbow lake. The name "oxbow" described the lake's U shape. In later years, however, the river returned to flow past Vicksburg.

After 18 years, the region near Vicksburg still showed signs of the Civil War. A battle had been fought there. From the boat deck, Sam saw trees crippled by cannon balls.

The approach to New Orleans was familiar to Sam. The water was up to the top of the levee. The embankment kept the water from flooding the flat country below. As the boat moved along on the high river, Sam looked down upon the houses and into the upper windows.

The old brick salt warehouses clustered at the upper end of the city looked the same as always. The vast plank wharves remained unchanged. There were as many ships as ever. But the steamboats were gone. Not one was left.

Although New Orleans had grown in size and population, it didn't really seem changed to Sam in other ways. Litter was still deep in the streets, and barrels sat all over the sidewalks. The great blocks of commercial buildings were as dusty as ever.

However, New Orleans seemed to be the best lighted city in the Union. Everyone was using gaslights, instead of oil lamps. Sam learned that the first cable for electric lights would be laid in the city within two years. And the telephone was everywhere!

Sam didn't stay long in New Orleans. He took the fastest packet going north. He was anxious to visit his boyhood home, Hannibal, Missouri.

It was nightfall when Sam passed the town of Louisiana,

Missouri. A sleepy village in his boyhood, it was part of a major railroad line now. All the towns, Sam discovered, had become part of the railroad line. He hardly recognized the places.

Sam reached Hannibal in the morning. As he stepped ashore, he felt as if he were returning home after having been in jail for years. The familiar and strange were mixed together. He saw new houses, and then remembered the old houses that used to be there.

He walked through the streets, and climbed a hill to get a better view. From the hill, he looked up and down the river and over to the wooded shore of Illinois. The river and woods

Samuel Clemens—Mark Twain—as he appeared in a photograph taken after 1859. (Missouri Historical Society)

looked the same. But Hannibal was changed. Remembering his boyhood, Sam felt the change.

He had been born in Missouri when it held slaves. He had seen the passing of the stagecoach, the Pony Express, and the steamboats on the river. He had seen the country fight a civil war.

Now he lived in a country that was building railroads. Major routes led from the Mississippi to the east, to the south, and to the west coast. Sam could board a train at Hannibal and ride to Chicago or Burlington, Iowa. Hannibal was no longer a steamboat town. It was a railroad town.

To Sam it seemed that the entire Mississippi River Valley was fast becoming an industrial center. Soon tall wooden poles strung with telephone wires and electric cables would line the riverbanks.

Everyone along the river was busy planning how they could use the river to make money, and then more money. Sam concluded that something very important was missing from American life. But what? If he could only know what it was.

As Sam left the Mississippi and returned to his New England home, he felt helpless and lonely. He was glad he wouldn't live long enough to see more changes along the river. As it was, he had already seen too much. How he longed for the life he once knew on the Mississippi!

6

Journey of the Towboat Captain

1943

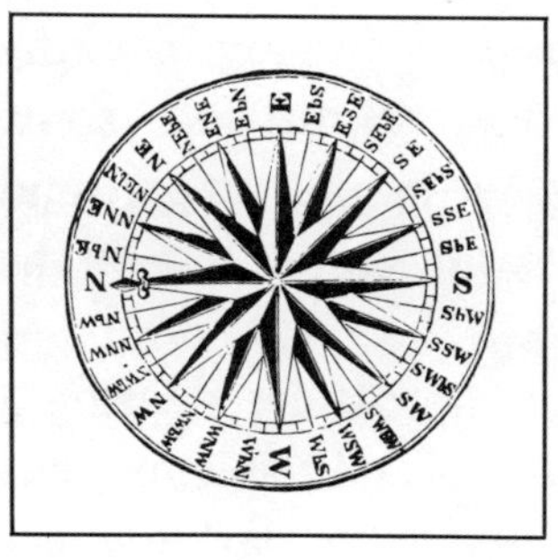

Had Sam lived seven more years, he would have seen riverboats come back to the Mississippi. In 1917, the federal government created the Federal Barge Lines. A barge was a floating steel box, 175 feet long, designed to slide through the water easily while carrying a load of about 1500 tons. A riverboat again became the easiest, cheapest, and safest way to move a heavy load.

It was December 1, 1943, and the United States was fighting World War II. Coming to push some of the great barges was Captain Samuel Mack of the towboat *Whistle*. His load was war equipment—tanks, cannons, and small armored scout cars

—manufactured at the government arsenal in Rock Island, Illinois.

From the pilothouse (the room from which the boat is steered), Captain Mack spotted his shipment. The barges he was going to move were together. The tow consisted of three barges linked end-to-end by cables to form a straight line.

Captain Mack pulled up to the tow. Quickly, two deckhands lashed the barges to the towboat in the zero temperature. To add to their difficulty, the wind was blowing an icy spray onto the barges. In a few more days, ice would seal this part of the river and leave it flowing beneath its frozen cover.

"Get another set of cables on that tank barge!" ordered Captain Mack. His voice sounded harsh as it came over the squawk box from the pilothouse. "The ice is already blocking the water flow at St. Louis. We're going to run into some shallow spots. That barge is loaded deep. We might run aground and break up the whole tow. I sure don't want barges lost on the Mississippi."

At the head of the tow, a Navy petty officer wearing a heavy fur parka, face mask, and goggles guarded the shipment. His pistol, tucked inside a holster, was under his parka where the icy spray wouldn't freeze it.

"No chance of loosing a barge, is there?" he asked a deckhand.

"You heard the Captain," snapped the deckhand. "Wouldn't be the first time he lost a barge."

The petty officer looked worried. He was to ride on the towboat all the way to New Orleans, standing guard duty on and off every half an hour. He worked six-hour shifts.

Suddenly, the Captain's voice blasted through the squawk box again. "Hey! Get a life jacket on that sailor!"

In the pilothouse, Captain Mack talked to himself. "Since when do I outfit Navy men with life jackets! Look at that temperature. Zero! Those barges are caked with ice and I've got a sailor aboard without a life jacket. He falls overboard and he's dead. That icy water will sap his strength. With a jacket, he's got a chance of coming up alive."

An hour later, the tow was connected to the *Whistle.* Captain Mack backed up the boat and her tow of three tightly lashed barges. In a few minutes, the towboat was in the channel.

"This tow isn't stopping!" the Captain bellowed over the squawk box to his crew of ten. "From here on out, it's full power ahead unless we run aground."

But the tow did stop below Rock Island. At 3 p.m., the *Whistle* moved into a lock chamber on the high side of a dam. Gates closed electrically behind the towboat, sealing her off from the water on the high side. She sat still while water flowed out of the lock through special openings. When the water in the lock chamber was low enough, the gates on the low side of the dam opened and the *Whistle* left the lock at 4:45.

This lock was just one of many that the *Whistle* would enter. Between the Falls of St. Anthony at Minneapolis, Minnesota, and the mouth of the Ohio River was a vast system of dams and locks. Their purpose was to maintain an adequate depth of water for barges to pass through. Otherwise, barges wouldn't be able to use the Mississippi during periods when the river level dropped.

These locks and dams, built in the 1930s, had changed

Barges and a towboat are lowered in Lock No. 1 at Minneapolis, Minnesota. From here to the mouth of the Ohio are 27 locks. (Minnesota Historical Society/Steve Plattner)

the Mississippi into a chain of lakes. The upper part of the river was now a series of "steps" that boats could either "climb" or "go down" as they traveled upstream, or downstream.

Farther south, the petty officer heard the sound of train wheels racing on a track. Then, a long, shrill whistle pierced the air. He looked up to watch a puffing steam locomotive and 18 cars cross a railroad bridge over the river at Fort Madison, Iowa. All the way across the bridge, the cars squeaked and whined. It sounded as if the whole bridge would collapse and fall into the river.

But the bridge held the train. It was a troop train, packed

with soldiers. The Navy man on the tow wondered if the train were bound for a basic-training base, or a port from which the men would be shipped overseas to a battlefield.

From the pilothouse, Captain Mack watched the train and said a silent prayer for the soldiers aboard. He thought of his son at war. It was a sad thought that was always with him.

On December 2, the *Whistle* reached the mouth of the Missouri River. Now the blue waters of the Mississippi merged with the muddy waters of the Missouri. The Mississippi appeared to be two different rivers flowing in the same waterway. Along one bank, the waters were blue. On the other side, the waters were brown. Eventually, the entire river became muddy with silt the Missouri had brought.

As the crew sat down for dinner later that afternoon, the temperature outside was still zero. By 7 p.m., the second watch (the crew who worked the midnight to 6 a.m. shift) was in the galley drinking coffee. Some played pinochle until they were ready to go to work.

Now it was completely dark in the pilothouse, except for the small light above the steering levers. The big hands on the levers were those of Officer Dick Penn, who commanded the towboat while Captain Mack was sleeping.

Outside, heavy clouds covered the moon and stars. The only lights were from the great searchlights on the pilothouse roof, the red lights along the left sides of the barges and towboat, and the green lights along their right sides.

The searchlights swept through the night, first to the barges ahead, then to the Coast day-mark (a river mileage marker posted on the bank), to a red buoy, to a black buoy, then back to the barges. As the searchlights flashed across the water, Mr. Penn spotted a clump of brush in the water. When he came up river three days ago, the channel ran along the other side of the brush. Now it had changed and swung way over to the other shore. Must tell the Captain, he thought, so the buoys can be moved. This river changes so fast that it's hard to keep track of its route.

Following the buoys which marked the path of the channel, Mr. Penn zigzagged the towboat back and forth across the river. The main channel was actually a narrow strip of deep water bordered by shallow side channels, islands, lakes, and sloughs (small muddy marshlands).

Much of the channel had been made by the U.S. Army Corps of Engineers. The river bottom had been dug

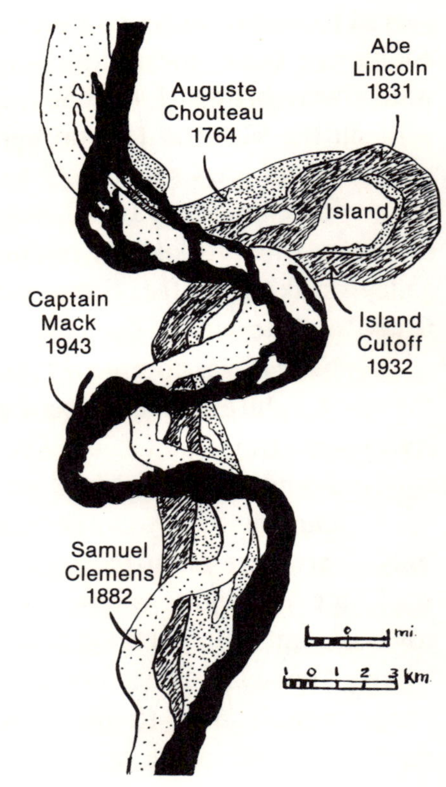

A section of the river showing how the Mississippi has changed from 1764 to 1943. (Map by Mauri Formigoni)

out, the banks lined with rocks, and the curves straightened. In some places, the Mississippi was so walled up that it couldn't spread out anymore. When heavy rains came, the river rose and spilled into the surrounding countryside.

Mr. Penn claimed that navigating a towboat on the Mississippi was as difficult as in the old steamboat days. As in Sam Clemens's time, a river pilot must know the Mississippi by heart and keep his river knowledge up-to-date. Pilots read weekly reports about the Mississippi provided by the Army Corps, and talked with other river pilots over the radio.

All night, the *Whistle* moved downstream, guided by the powerful searchlights. Mr. Penn didn't make one mistake. One error and a barge would run aground, or scrape river bottom. Then, the barge cables would break, and free all the barges to float downstream until picked up by other boats.

Mr. Penn's job was even more dangerous now that the United States was at war. The government feared that the barges might be bombed by saboteurs, or enemy agents. As a result, an armed soldier guarded each bridge.

At midnight, Mr. Penn was relieved by Captain Mack. The petty officer guarding the tow gave up his watch to a deckhand, and headed for bed.

At 6 a.m., December 3, Mr. Penn returned to the pilothouse. It was getting daylight about 40 minutes later, and he switched off the searchlights. Outside, it was two above zero. For several hundred feet, the *Whistle* slid through silt and chunks of ice.

Late that day, the towboat reached the mouth of the

A towboat arrives at the junction of the Ohio and Mississippi rivers. The red marker on the bank signals the joining of the rivers. The darker shading on the left is actually blue water mingling with the darker muddy Mississippi.(*Photo by John and Maxine Nolan*)

Ohio River where the blue waters of the Ohio mingled with the dirty brown Mississippi. Below the Ohio, the Mississippi was known as the Lower Mississippi. Above the Ohio, the river was called the Upper Mississippi.

From now on, it was open water—no locks or dams—to New Orleans. Because the river flowed wide below the Ohio, there was more river traffic. A fast warship passed the *Whistle,* headed for New Orleans. Other barges loaded with war supplies were being pushed by towboats similar to the *Whistle.*

By now, the *Whistle* was beginning to run low on fuel.

Below Memphis, Tennessee, a refueling barge pulled up along the towboat. Hoses were connected to the fuel tank, and 25,000 gallons of oil were pumped aboard. The *Whistle* used about 3,600 gallons of oil a day, and her tanks held 28,000 gallons.

Two days later, the *Whistle* passed Vicksburg. By removing earth and digging a nine-mile canal, engineers had turned the Mississippi and made it flow, once again, beside the city. Its waters were gentle here and made Vicksburg an excellent harbor. It was so warm—58 degrees—that Captain Mack shed his jacket and threw open the window of the pilothouse.

Captain Mack steers safely past a long line of barges at Vicksburg, Mississippi. (Photo by John and Maxine Nolan)

That afternoon, the *Whistle* went by Baton Rouge, capital of Louisiana. The banks were lined with chemical factories. Factory wastes, such as used chemicals and pieces of metal, were polluting the water. The city was also using the river as a sewerage outlet, and this polluted the water even more.

The towboat continue downstream and pulled into a landing north of New Orleans. The *Whistle* was exactly on time: December 10. Quickly, the deckhands unlashed the tow and stashed the cables in piles on the deck. Great cranes lifted the war equipment onto waiting liberty ships. These vessels were called "liberty" ships because their supplies were supposed to bring liberty to those countries at war.

At 6 p.m., the *Whistle* tied up at the landing point. The petty officer who had ridden all the way from Rock Island reported to his new assignment aboard a destroyer-escort. He was bound for the South Pacific. Captain Mack who lived near New Orleans packed his clothes and headed for his home by bus. He would spend Christmas Day on the river, as the *Whistle* was scheduled to pull out of New Orleans on December 12, pushing another tow.

7

Today's Journey
1980

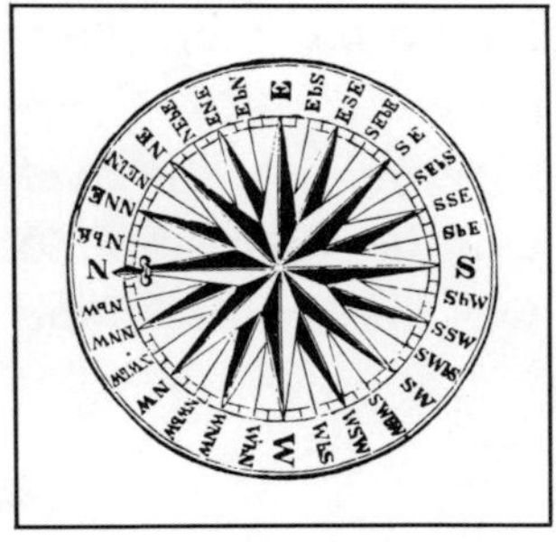

"Untie the lines, Mark!" Dave Oxford shouted. "We're taking off!"

Eleven-year-old Mark did not hear his father's call. His eyes were fixed on the lock master who was riding a bicycle along the high concrete side of Lock No. 17, south of Muscatine, Iowa, on the Mississippi. The man was pedaling to help a boat which was about to enter the lock.

The houseboat that Mark's parents had rented, No. 28, had been inside the lock only a few minutes. The lines which the lock master had thrown down were attached to cleats (metal supports on the walls). Mark had wound the free ends of the ropes around the cleats at the front and back of the boat. Once tied, the lines kept the houseboat from being smashed against the sides of the lock while the water level was lowered about two feet.

"Mark!"

This time Mark heard. He untied the lines, and his father steered through the lock chamber until the gates closed behind.

Standing on the deck of the houseboat, Mark gazed out at the river. It looked as if they were crossing a large lake, not a river. On either side, the Mississippi branched out into two wide arms. Speedboats, sailboats, and a canoe cruised the shining silver waters.

Mark's parents, who took turns steering the boat, followed the marked channel. They kept to the red buoys on the starboard (right side) and the green or black buoys on the port (left side). They also had a chart which showed the main channel, towns, marinas, islands, locks and dams.

Mark wished he could travel all 2,552 miles of the river from Lake Itasca in Minnesota, the source of the Mississippi, to the Gulf of Mexico. His friend Jimmy was aboard the *Delta*

From the cold blue waters of Lake Itasca in Minnesota, a clear, shallow stream runs out of the forest. The stream is the beginning of the Mississippi River. (Minnesota Conservation Department/Walter H. Wettschreck)

Mark followed the winding curves of the Mississippi as it flowed through fields and woods north of New Orleans. (Photographic Service Corp./ Tom Owen)

Queen steamboat, following the river from St. Louis to New Orleans, then back again. Mark was only going from his home in Muscatine to south of St. Louis. His father, who was working on a Mississippi River pollution project for the federal government, was combining business with pleasure on their summer vacation.

Mark wandered to the rear of the boat where his sister, Debbie, was flying a kite.

"Being on a houseboat is boring," she complained. Debbie, age 10, was a chubby girl with dark brown hair.

"If a storm strikes us in the middle of the river, it won't be boring," Mark said.

"There's no storm, only the hot sun and bugs!" Debbie snapped. She swatted an insect crawling up her arm. "I don't know why dad had to take this houseboat trip to see how polluted the river is. Anyone can see it's dirty. Just look at that!"

Debbie pointed to a large foamy patch floating in the water. Bottles, a soccer ball, and other trash bobbed in the water.

The Mississippi, which drained a third of the United States's waterways, was an enormous garbage dump. Rivers flowing into it brought wastes from chemical, industrial, sewage, and atomic power plants. The Mississippi also picked up pollutants from the cities, factories, and power plants which it passed.

In many places along the Mississippi and those rivers empting into it, crops were planted right up to the banks. Fertilizers, pesticides, and herbicides which farmers used to grow more crops and protect them from insects and weeds ran off

The federal government's Landsat satellite can follow the course of garbage, trash, and industrial wastes dumped into the Mississippi. This view shows the Mississippi from St. Louis, Missouri to Greenville, Mississippi, some 570 miles above Earth. St. Louis (A) is about 20 miles south of the mouth of the Missouri River (B) which empties into the Mississippi (C). The Illinois River (D) flows into the Mississippi to the west. (NASA)

Debris floats along the shore of the Mississippi. (Photo by El Rancho)

into the rivers when it rained. These chemicals added their poisons to the rivers and killed water life. Factories which made fertilizers were built along the Mississippi and polluted the air with dust and gases.

Suddenly, eight barges pushed by a towboat slid dangerously close to the houseboat. Mr. Oxford steered away just in time. Mark and Debbie grasped the deck railing as waves rolled over their feet.

"We could have been killed!" Mrs. Oxford exclaimed to her husband.

He shook his head. "They came too fast," he explained. "The captain of that tow should be reported." He switched on the two-way radio to tell the lock master at Lock No. 18 about the incident. Following his report, he was informed that a barge was using the lock. If he wanted to come through, he would have to wait four hours.

"Four hours!" Debbie wailed. She wrapped a wet towel around her neck to cool off. It was 103 degrees.

"If you find a cool place to wait, let me know," her mother joked.

Five hot hours later the lock master radioed for Houseboat No. 28 to move ahead. They passed into the lock and down another water level.

As the first day of their cruise neared its end, the Oxford family started looking for a spot to spend the night. They found a good place along the Illinois shoreline. In a quiet and shallow inlet far from the main channel, they dropped anchor.

While Mrs. Oxford cooked supper on the electric stove,

Debbie waves to a passing speedboat from the top of Houseboat No. 28, anchored along the Illinois shoreline. (Illinois Office of Tourism/ Michael Scott)

Debbie swam, Mark and his dad fished. Mark caught a crappie and then noticed a large catfish resting in the water along the bank. He reached down and picked it up. The fish lay limp in his hand, its eyes covered with silt.

"What's wrong with this fish, Dad?" Mark asked.

His father took the fish and examined it. "Looks as if silt is blocking its vision," he explained. "When that happens, the fish becomes confused because it can't see very well. It comes to the surface and sometimes boat propellers run over and kill it."

Mr. Oxford poured a little water over the catfish's eyes

to wash away the silt, then tossed it back in the river. He also recorded information about the fish in a notebook.

"What makes the Mississippi so muddy?" Mark asked.

"It's always been muddy because of erosion," his father explained. "But these back areas are filling up with silt because of the barge traffic. As barges move, they draw tons of water with them. The water turns up silt along the channel and dumps it on islands and into side channels and sloughs. Silt is robbing water plants of sunlight. As the plants die, animal life in the water dies, too."

"If silt blinds the catfish," Mark reasoned, "then why does the government allow barges on the river?"

His father looked surprised. "You don't realize how important barge traffic is. The power plant in our town, for example, burns coal to make electricity. The coal comes there by barge."

Mark knew that burning coal polluted the air and water. They had discussed it in class. His father had also explained that the power plant used water from the Mississippi to cool off its condensers. When the water was dumped back into the river, it was steaming hot. The hot water, or thermal pollution, killed or harmed fish and plants in the Mississippi.

"Without coal to run the power plant," his dad continued, "you would live in a house without heat, hot water, and electricity. Do you think you'd like that?"

"I guess not," admitted Mark. "But couldn't trucks or trains bring our coal?"

"Sure. But one barge carries as much cargo as sixty

trucks or fifteen train cars. A barge is the best way to move heavy loads. More and more barges use the river every year so the Mississippi becomes muddier."

"And the catfish becomes blind," broke in Mark.

"Yes," his father answered. "Part of my job is to find out how barge traffic, industries, and the whole big Mississippi can survive together. No one understands how all living things—plants and animals—in the river are affected by silt and other kinds of pollution. Our research team must decide how barge traffic and industries will have to change so that living things can continue to exist in the river."

"What if it's too late for those changes? What if everything in the Mississippi dies?"

His father shook his head sadly. "That might happen," he admitted. "Changes might come too late. But, are you willing to give up your heated home, television, radio, hot showers, and electric lights so that catfish can see?"

Mark frowned at his father. He didn't know if he really wanted to give up all those things! He still didn't know when Debbie yelled from inside the boat. They ran into the bathroom where they found Debbie and her mother staring into a sink full of black water.

"I wanted to wash my hair and the water is black!" cried Debbie.

"Somehow that sink isn't hooked up to the boat's water tanks," her father concluded. "What you have there is Mississippi River water."

"Sick!" exclaimed Debbie.

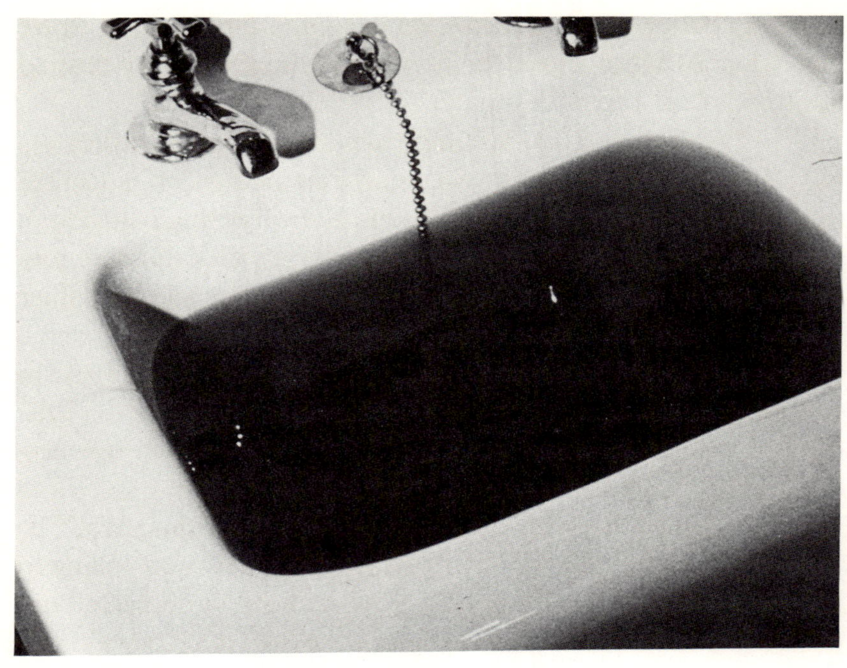

Water from the Mississippi River flowing into this sink was black, polluted by silt. (Photo by John and Maxine Nolan)

Within an hour, the pipes from the sink were connected to the tanks. Now the water ran clear into the sink.

No wonder the catfish has trouble living in the Mississippi, thought Mark. I bet people have problems cleaning up that water!

Mark had already noticed many purification plants along the banks. In fact, most communities along the Mississippi used the river for their drinking water. At water treatment plants, chemicals were added to the water to remove silt and kill bacteria. Better ways were needed to purify the drinking water and rid it of all its many pollutants, especially cancer-causing agents.

That evening, as the family watched the river reflect the purple and pink colors of the setting sun, Mark and Debbie asked what they could do to help clean up the Mississippi.

"You can pick up trash and garbage along the river and don't throw litter into the water or along the banks," their mother suggested.

"And make a report on water pollution in school so other people will become concerned about pollution in the Mississippi," their dad added. "People need to know how pollution affects them, and become more involved in developing ideas and plans which will better help living things exist in the river."

Laying in their bunks that night, the Mississippi rocked Mark and Debbie, gently lapping its water against the hull. They decided to organize a clean-up group among their friends and pick up litter along the river near their home.

Eight locks more, and the houseboat passed the mouth of the Missouri River. The water coming from the Missouri was gray, not brown. Large dams on the river, which were used to control flooding, had cleaned up the river. The dams filtered out silt by stopping the water flow. When the water speed was zero, silt dropped to the river bottom. The "clean" water then spilled over to the next dam. When it reached the Mississippi, the water carried very little silt.

South of the Missouri's mouth, the houseboat cruised by

St. Louis. Barges loaded with coal, fertilizer, and grain crowded the channel. Mark looked up to the Gateway Arch at the Jefferson Expansion Memorial along the river, where Rene Auguste Chouteau had chopped down that first tree to build the city which had become the "Gateway to the West."

By now, Mark was wishing that their houseboat trip was over. It was so hot—109 degrees! The wind, ruffling his dark

The Gateway Arch in St. Louis honors Thomas Jefferson's purchase of Louisiana, and the movement of pioneers from the eastern United States to the West. In the top of the Arch is an observation room, 630 feet above the ground. (Illinois State Historical Library)

hair, felt like a blast from an oven. Countless times, they had stopped at marinas for ice and soft drinks.

Over the radio came the announcement that the Mississippi was closed at Dubuque, Iowa. Because the Midwest summer was so hot and dry, the river level had dropped drastically. Barges were stuck in the mud north of Dubuque!

Another report told about twelve tons of dangerous chemicals which had spilled into the river near Shell Beach, Louisiana. The bags of chemicals had been knocked into the water when two ships collided. Now these chemicals were polluting the water and harming water life. Fishing in the area was forbidden.

From St. Louis, the river flowed five miles wide between tall bluffs. They cruised down to a sandy area along the western bank. Already two houseboats and five speedboats were on the beach. Houseboat No. 28 anchored on the sand.

After a swim, Mark and Debbie explored the area. Along the water's edge, they picked up a few pieces of limestone, then quickly dropped them. Underneath the rocks were scorpions, their long tails curving, raising up to strike them. Mark stepped back just in time. Debbie didn't. A scorpion struck her foot. She screamed and ran wildly back to the houseboat. Mark followed close behind. Immediately, their mother put ammonia on the wound.

"Lucky for you those were stripe-backed scorpions," she told Debbie. "Their poison will only make your foot hurt and swell."

"Are you sure?" Debbie wailed. "I thought scorpions killed you!"

A stripe-back scorpion raises its tail to strike. These scorpions are found along the Mississippi from south of St. Louis to Louisiana. (Illinois State Museum)

"Not these," her mother assured her.

Debbie sat on a deck chair. To keep down the swelling, she put her foot into a bucket filled with cold water. Near the boat prowled the most common animal found along the Mississippi—a muskrat.

Debbie groaned. She didn't want to see any more animals.

Early the next morning, the Oxfords awoke to see the *Delta Queen* pushing her way up river. The *Queen* and her sister ship, the *Mississippi Queen,* were the only passenger steamboats left on the Mississippi. People living along the river

The paddlewheel pushes the *Delta Queen* up river, following the Mississippi from New Orleans to St. Paul, Minnesota. The *Queen* also travels the Ohio River from its mouth to Gallipolis, Ohio. (Photo by John and Maxine Nolan)

telephoned each other to report each ship's progress up and down the waterway. No one wanted to miss seeing the last of these great steamboats.

"Jimmy! Hey, Jimmy!" Mark shouted from the deck. With binoculars, he had spotted his friend jogging along the *Queen*'s deck. But Jimmy didn't hear Mark's cries. He was too far away.

"That lucky Jimmy!" Mark exclaimed. "He gets air-conditioning and a movie theater."

"I'd rather be on the *Mississippi Queen*," said Debbie, limping up behind him on her swollen foot. "It has a swimming pool."

"Who cares? As long as it's air-conditioned," said Mark.

That morning, the family headed back to Muscatine. Going against the current took more time than they had thought. Their arrival was a day late, but the man at the marina understood.

"I always add another day for beginners," he explained. "Next trip, you'll arrive on time."

As they left the marina in their car, Mark looked back at the river and wondered if Jimmy were home yet. He was going to enlist him in their clean-up project, since he, Debbie, and Jimmy were all veterans of journeys on the Mississippi.

Index